MW01140629

WASTE MANAGEMENT: THE GLOBAL VIEW
Managing Our Waste Series

• • • • • • • • • • • • • • • • • •

Written by Erika Gasper Gombatz, M.A.

GRADES 5 - 8
Reading Levels 3 - 4

Classroom Complete Press

P.O. Box 19729
San Diego, CA 92159
Tel: 1-800-663-3609 / Fax: 1-800-663-3608
Email: service@classroomcompletepress.com

www.classroomcompletepress.com

ISBN-13: 978-1-55319-305-0
ISBN-10: 1-55319-305-9

© 2007

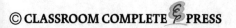

Critical Thinking Skills

Waste Management: The Global View

Skills For Critical Thinking	Section 1	Section 2	Section 3	Section 4	Section 5	Section 6	Section 7	Section 8	Hands-on Activities
LEVEL 1 Knowledge									
• List Details/Facts	✓	✓	✓	✓	✓	✓	✓	✓	✓
• Recall Information	✓	✓	✓	✓	✓	✓	✓	✓	
• Match Vocab. to Definitions	✓				✓	✓	✓		
• Define Vocabulary	✓		✓	✓	✓	✓	✓	✓	
• Recognize Validity (T/F)	✓			✓		✓			
LEVEL 2 Comprehension									
• Demonstrate Understanding	✓	✓	✓	✓	✓	✓	✓	✓	✓
• Explain Scientific Causation	✓	✓	✓	✓	✓	✓	✓	✓	✓
• Rephrasing Vocab. Meaning	✓		✓	✓			✓	✓	
• Describe	✓	✓	✓	✓	✓	✓	✓	✓	✓
• Classify Objects Into Groups		✓		✓		✓			
LEVEL 3 Application									
• Application to Own Life	✓	✓	✓	✓	✓	✓	✓	✓	✓
• Model Scientific Process	✓	✓	✓	✓	✓	✓	✓	✓	✓
• Organize & Classify Facts		✓	✓	✓		✓			
• Use Alternative Research Tools	✓	✓	✓	✓	✓	✓	✓	✓	✓
LEVEL 4 Analysis									
• Distinguish Meanings	✓			✓			✓	✓	
• Make Inferences	✓	✓	✓	✓	✓	✓	✓	✓	✓
• Draw Conclusions Based on Facts Provided	✓	✓	✓	✓	✓	✓	✓	✓	✓
• Classify Based on Facts Researched		✓	✓	✓		✓		✓	✓
• Sequence Events		✓		✓	✓				
LEVEL 5 Synthesis									
• Compile Research Information	✓	✓	✓	✓	✓	✓	✓	✓	✓
• Design & Application						✓	✓	✓	✓
• Create & Construct			✓		✓				
• Imagine Self in Scientific Role	✓	✓	✓	✓		✓	✓		✓
LEVEL 6 Evaluation									
• State & Defend an Opinion	✓	✓	✓	✓	✓	✓	✓	✓	✓
• Evaluate Best Practices	✓	✓	✓	✓	✓	✓	✓	✓	✓
• Make Recommendations	✓	✓	✓	✓	✓	✓	✓	✓	✓
• Influence Community	✓	✓	✓	✓	✓	✓	✓	✓	✓

Based on Bloom's Taxonomy

Contents

Assessment Rubric

• • • • • • • • • • • • • • • • • • •

Waste Management: The Global View

Student's Name: _____ Assignment: _____ Level: _____

	Level 1	Level 2	Level 3	Level 4
Understanding Concepts	Demonstrates a limited understanding of concepts. Requires Teacher intervention.	Demonstrates a basic understanding of concepts. Requires little teacher intervention.	Demonstrates a good understanding of concepts. Requires no teacher intervention.	Demonstrates a thorough understanding of concepts. Requires no teacher intervention.
Analysis & Application of Key Concepts	Limited application and interpretation in activity responses	Basic application and interpretation in activity responses	Good application and interpretation in activity responses	Strong application and interpretation in activity responses
Creativity & Imagination	Limited creativity and imagination applied in projects and activities	Some creativity and imagination applied in projects and activities	Satisfactory level of creativity and imagination applied in projects and activities	Beyond expected creativity and imagination applied in projects and activities

STRENGTHS:

WEAKNESSES:

NEXT STEPS:

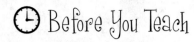

Teacher Guide

Our resource has been created for ease of use by both **TEACHERS** *and* **STUDENTS** *alike.*

Introduction

Our resource provides ready-to-use information and activities for remedial students in grades five to eight. Written to grade and using simplified language and vocabulary, SOCIAL STUDIES concepts are presented in a way that makes them more accessible to students and easier to understand. Comprised of reading passages, student activities and overhead transparencies, our resource can be used effectively for whole-class, small group and independent work.

How Is Our Resource Organized?

STUDENT HANDOUTS

Reading passages and **activities** (in the form of reproducible worksheets) make up the majority of our resource. The reading passages present important grade-appropriate information and concepts related to the topic. Embedded in each passage are one or more questions that ensure students understand what they have read.

For each reading passage there are BEFORE YOU READ activities and AFTER YOU READ activities.

- The BEFORE YOU READ activities prepare students for reading by setting a purpose for reading. They stimulate background knowledge and experience, and guide students to make connections between what they know and what they will learn. Important concepts and vocabulary are also presented.

- The AFTER YOU READ activities check students' comprehension of the concepts presented in the reading passage and extend their learning. Students are asked to give thoughtful consideration of the reading passage through creative and evaluative short-answer questions, research, and extension activities.

Hands-On Activities are included to further develop students' thinking skills and understanding of the concepts. The **Assessment Rubric** (*page 4*) is a useful tool for evaluating students' responses to many of the activities in our resource. The **Comprehension Quiz** (*page 48*) can be used for either a follow-up review or assessment at the completion of the unit.

PICTURE CUES

Our resource contains three main types of pages, each with a different purpose and use. A Picture Cue at the top of each page shows, at a glance, what the page is for.

 Teacher Guide
- Information and tools for the teacher

 Student Handouts
- Reproducible worksheets and activities

 Easy Marking™ Answer Key
- Answers for student activities

EASY MARKING™ ANSWER KEY

Marking students' worksheets is fast and easy with this **Answer Key**. Answers are listed in columns – just line up the column with its corresponding worksheet, as shown, and see how every question matches up with its answer!

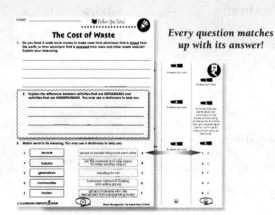

Every question matches up with its answer!

Bloom's Taxonomy

Our resource is an effective tool for any SOCIAL STUDIES PROGRAM.

Bloom's Taxonomy* for Reading Comprehension

The activities in our resource engage and build the full range of thinking skills that are essential for students' reading comprehension and understanding of important SOCIAL STUDIES concepts. Based on the six levels of thinking in Bloom's Taxonomy, and using language at a remedial level, information and questions are given that challenge students to not only recall what they have read, but move beyond this to understand the text and concepts through higher-order thinking. By using higher-order skills of application, analysis, synthesis and evaluation, students become active readers, drawing more meaning from the text, attaining a greater understanding of concepts, and applying and extending their learning in more sophisticated ways.

Our resource, therefore, is an effective tool for any SOCIAL STUDIES program. Whether it is used in whole or in part, or adapted to meet individual student needs, our resource provides teachers with essential information and questions to ask, inspiring students' interest, creativity, and promoting meaningful learning.

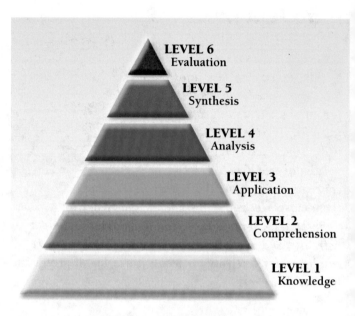

**BLOOM'S TAXONOMY:
6 LEVELS OF THINKING**

*Bloom's Taxonomy is a widely used tool by educators for classifying learning objectives, and is based on the work of Benjamin Bloom.

Vocabulary

acid	agricultural	algae	atoms	bacteria
bio-economical	biology	biomass	communications	contaminate
cyanide	debris	disaster	earthquake	economics
ecosystem	environment	ethanol	factories	fuel rod
fungi	fungicide	generations	groundwater	hazardous
herbicide	hurricane	incinerator	landfill	missions
nuclear	nucleus	nutrients	oil slick	oil tanker
orbit	ore	organic	oxygen	passengers
pesticide	phytoplankton	pollution	profits	radioactive
renewable resource	satellite	sewage	sustainable	syringes
technologies	telescope	tornadoes	toxic	tsunami
unsustainable	uranium	waste	wastewater	zero waste

Agricultural Waste

1. Think about a farm. What types of waste do you think might be produced on the farm?

_____

_____

_____

2. Use a dictionary to look up the word AGRICULTURAL. Write the definition on the lines below.

The definition of **agricultural** is:

_____

_____

_____

3. Match word to its definition. You may use a dictionary to help you.

1	disease	the natural home of a living thing — A
2	habitat	substances that living things need to live and grow — B
3	environment	a harmful condition in which the body is not working properly — C
4	bacteria	a resource that is replaced as fast as it is used — D
5	nutrients	tiny living things — E
6	renewable	everything that surrounds you — F

📖 Reading Passage

Agricultural Waste

What is agricultural waste?

We all need food to eat. Most of the food we eat comes from farms. Vegetables, grain, animals, and fruit are grown on farms around the world. But farms produce more than foods. They also produce a lot of waste. Waste from farms is called **agricultural waste**.

When you think of waste from a farm, you may first think of left over plant parts. In most cases, the vegetables, grains, and fruit that we eat are just a small part of a plant. After farmers pick the useful parts, a large amount of plant matter is left over. But plant matter is only one type of agricultural waste. Some farms use large amounts of **toxic**, or harmful, substances to kill plant pests and diseases, including:

- **pesticides**, substances that kill insect pests;
- **herbicides**, substances that kill plants, such as weeds;
- **fungicides**, substances that kill fungi, which can cause plant diseases.

Farms also use fertilizers, substances that make plants grow faster. When farmers water plants, some of these substances wash off. The water that does not get taken up by plants runs into creeks and streams, where these substances can harm the environment.

Describe the meaning of the term *agricultural waste*. Give three examples of agricultural waste.

_____

_____

How does agricultural waste cause harm?

When pesticides, herbicides, and fungicides wash off of farms and into the environment, these substances can be taken up by plants and animals. They can kill insects and plants in natural habitats and cause food chains to break down.

When fertilizers get into natural habitats, they can cause **algae** to grow out of control. The algae can block sunlight, and take up a lot of **oxygen**. This makes it hard for plants and animals to survive.

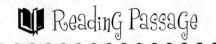

Agricultural Waste

How can we help lessen agricultural waste?

Different kinds of farms grow plants in different ways. Some farms grow a single type of crop plant every year. They may plant huge areas of just one crop. That crop takes the same **nutrients** out of the soil year after year. Insects that eat that type of plant come to the area in large numbers. Diseases that affect the plant, such as certain fungi and **bacteria**, can become a big problem since they can live on the same plant year after year. In order to grow the same crop year after year, the farm must use a lot of fertilizers, pesticides, and fungicides.

Other kinds of farms are run differently. Many farmers have gone back to older ways of farming, where many different kinds of plants are grown together in the same area. Farmers grow plants that draw in, or attract, animals that feed on crop-eating insects. Farmers grow different plants each year, so that the same nutrients are not taken out of the soil every year. Special plants that add nutrients to the soil grow between crop plants. Farmers compost plant waste to add more nutrients back to the soil. This type of farming is **sustainable**. The farm can produce crops year after year without having to add a lot of fertilizers or pesticides. If a farm uses no harmful pesticides or fertilizers, the crops can be labeled **organic**. Buying organic foods is one way people can lessen the amount of harmful agricultural waste in the environment.

Describe the meaning of the term *organic* when it is used to describe crops.

_____

_____

How can agricultural waste be useful?

After a crop is picked, farm fields may be covered with large amounts of plant waste, such as stalks, leaves, and roots. Plant waste is sometimes called **biomass**. People are now finding ways to make fuel from biomass.

Ethanol is a fuel made from the wasted parts of corn. Ethanol can be used to run cars and trucks. Other types of biomass fuels can be used to heat homes or burned in power plants to make electricity. Biomass is a **renewable resource**. It creates less pollution than burning **fossil fuels**. And, using biomass for fuel helps farmers get rid of waste and make money at the same time.

After You Read

NAME: _____

Agricultural Waste

1. **Circle** the word **TRUE** if the statement is TRUE **or** **Circle** the word **FALSE** if it is FALSE.

   A) Stalks and leaves can be agricultural waste.

          TRUE   **FALSE**

   B) Pesticides help plants grow faster.

          TRUE   **FALSE**

   C) Ethanol is a fuel made from unused parts of corn plants.

          TRUE   **FALSE**

   D) Biomass fuel is made from petroleum oil.

          TRUE   **FALSE**

   E) Organic crops are grown without pesticides, herbicides or fungicides.

          TRUE   **FALSE**

2. **Put a check mark (✓) next to the answer that is most correct.**

   a) **Which of these is used to kill insects that eat plants?**

   - ⚪ **A** pesticide
   - ⚪ **B** fertilizer
   - ⚪ **C** ethanol
   - ⚪ **D** fungicide

   b) **Which type of agricultural waste can be made into fuel?**

   - ⚪ **A** herbicide
   - ⚪ **B** biomass
   - ⚪ **C** nutrients
   - ⚪ **D** algae

   c) **What gets used up when the same crop is planted in the same place every year?**

   - ⚪ **A** oxygen
   - ⚪ **B** nutrients
   - ⚪ **C** biomass
   - ⚪ **D** pesticides

   d) **Which of these could cause algae to grow out of control?**

   - ⚪ **A** fungicides
   - ⚪ **B** biomass
   - ⚪ **C** pesticides
   - ⚪ **D** fertilizer

Agricultural Waste

3. **How would you explain sustainable farming in your own words?**

_____

_____

_____

4. **Do all types of agricultural wastes create the same problems? Use examples to explain your answer.**

_____

_____

_____

Extension & Application

5. Learn more about **organic farming**. Use the Internet or library resources to find answers to the questions below.

- How do organic farms differ from other farms?
- What are the rules for being labeled organic?

Then, look for nearby organic farms using your local business directory. Call the farm and ask to schedule a visit or a phone talk with a farmer. During your talk, ask the following questions:

- What types of crops do you grow on your farm?
- How do you protect your crops from being eaten by insects?
- How do you control plant diseases?
- How do you make sure your plants get enough nutrients?
- Write **at least two** more questions that you would like to ask when you talk to the farmer.

Create a slide show presentation to share what you learned with your class. The first slide should contain the name of the farm that you called or visited. The second slide should contain information about what the farm grows. Additional slides should contain answers to all of the questions you asked. Include photographs or images.

For each slide, write a note of what you want to say when you show that slide.

Give your slide show presentation to your class!

Waste from Mining

1. Think of a shiny metal. Now, think of a rock. Metal comes from rock. What do you think must be done to the rock to get just the metal?

_____

_____

_____

2. Use a dictionary to look up the terms ORE and ACID. Write the definitions on the lines below.

a) The definition of **ore** is: _____

_____

_____

b) The definition of **acid** is: _____

_____

_____

3. **Think of *FIVE* things that you used today that contain metal or other ores.**

1) _____

2) _____

3) _____

4) _____

5) _____

NAME: _____

Waste from Mining

What types of wastes are created from mining?

Mining for rocks, metals, and other **ores** creates huge amounts of waste. First, rock must be removed from the earth. Metals and other ores make up only a tiny part of rock. In order to get the ore, rock is first crushed, washed, sorted, and sometimes cooked. This process separates chunks that contain ore from chunks that do not. The rock that does not contain ore is waste. At this point, the waste material is not too harmful. It is a lot like the rock that was taken from the earth.

The next steps of mining create much more harmful, or **toxic**, waste. The metals we use in buildings, cars, and other products are very pure. In other words, they do not include any of the rock, only the metal. In many cases, mines use harmful substances such as **acid** and **cyanide** to separate the ore from the rock. When the metal is taken away, the leftover materials are very toxic.

Describe two different types of mining wastes.

_____

_____

How does mining waste cause harm?

Mining wastes can get into, or contaminate, huge areas around mines. Mining can go on for many years at one site. During that time, piles of rock and waste materials build up around the mine. Rain and snowmelt wash acids and other harmful substances into soil, ground water, lakes, and streams. Mine wastes can travel for many miles away from the mine.

Acids and other toxic waste from mines harm all kinds of living things. Mining waste can kill off plant life in an area. Animals must also move away, since they need plants to live. Mining waste has contaminated the drinking water supplies for many human communities, also.

NAME: _____

Waste from Mining

1. **Number the events from 1 to 5 in the order they occur in mining.**

_____ **a)** Acid is poured on the rock.

_____ **b)** Large amounts of rock are taken from the earth.

_____ **c)** Rock is sorted into pieces that contain ore and pieces that do not.

_____ **d)** Metals are removed from the rest of the rock materials.

_____ **e)** Rock is crushed and ground into small pieces.

---

2. **a)** ~~Cross out~~ **the words that are NOT waste products from mining**

  acid   biomass   cyanide   rock   oil

b) (Circle) **the places where mining waste can contaminate.**

  soil   well water   streams   the atmosphere   lakes

---

3. **Number the events from 1 to 4 in the order that they occur in mining.**

☐ **a)** piles of waste rock build up around the mine

☐ **b)** rain falls on the piles of rock

☐ **c)** acid and other harmful substances wash out of the rock pile

☐ **d)** mine waste contaminates water supply

14

NAME: _____

Waste from Mining

4. Explain how mining waste can travel many miles away from the mine.

_____

_____

_____

_____

5. Explain how people can be harmed by mining waste.

_____

_____

_____

_____

Extension & Application

6. Learn more about mine waste. Choose **one** of the topics listed below.

- **How do today's mines control their mining waste?**
- **How are old mines cleaned up?**

Check with your teacher if you would like to make up your own topic to research.

Then, use library or Internet resources to find information about your topic. After you have found some general information to answer your topic question, look for information to do a case study. A case study is a report about one example of your topic:

- If you are researching today's mines, look for information about **one mine that is in operation right now**. Find out how that mine controls its waste. Usually, a mine will have a website with information. Or, call the mine operator and ask for brochures or other print materials.

- If you are researching how old mines are cleaned up, look for information about **one clean-up operation**. Find out why the old mine was causing problems, and what steps people took to clean it up. Your local or regional environmental protection agency will have information about clean-up operations at old mines.

Before You Read

NAME: _____

Oil Spills

1. When you are at home, fill a bowl with water. Then, pour a small teaspoon of cooking oil into the bowl. Describe what happens.

_____

_____

_____

_____

2. Based on what happened to the oil in the bowl of water, what do you think happens to oil when it is spilled in the ocean?

_____

_____

_____

_____

_____

3. Use a dictionary to look up the term ECOSYSTEM. Write the definition on the lines below.

The definition of **ecosystem** is:

_____

_____

_____

_____

Oil Spills

What is the effect of oil spills?

Oil is shipped around the world by huge tankers. When tankers have accidents at sea, large amounts of oil can spill out. Oil floats on top of water, creating a film called an **oil slick**. The oil slick can travel on the surface of the water until it reaches the shore. When it does, the oil can cover places where animals live and have young.

Oil is very difficult to wash out of an environment. It sticks to soil and rocks. When oil covers birds, it sticks to their feathers and makes them unable to fly. Oil sticks to fishes' gills and makes them unable to breathe. Oil can kill eggs and young of many types of animals. Oil kills tiny floating plants called **phytoplankton**, which provide energy for all of the animals in the ocean ecosystem. An oil spill can be one of the worst disasters ever to happen in an ocean or near-shore habitat.

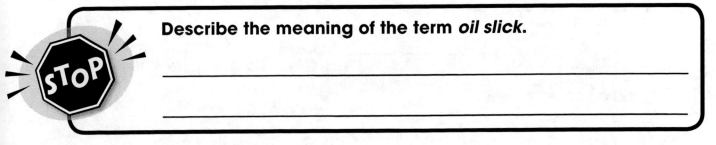

Describe the meaning of the term *oil slick*.

_____

_____

What is the *Exxon Valdez* oil spill?

In 1989, an oil tanker called the *Exxon Valdez* hit a reef off of the coast of Alaska. It spilled 11 million gallons of oil onto the water. The oil covered 1,300 miles of shoreline that was home to great numbers of wildlife, including bald eagles. The area of ocean covered by the spill was home to many types of fish and ocean mammals, including salmon, orcas, seals, otters, and whales. Huge numbers of animals were killed by the oil spill.

People worked hard to clean the area of oil. They washed oil off beaches with fire hoses. They cleaned off birds and mammals that they found still alive. But animals were killed in huge numbers, and it took many years for their populations to return to normal. Some species are still not back to the levels they were at before the spill. People suffered, too. The communities in the area depended on fishing, hunting, and tourism to make money. After the spill, none of these activities could take place for years. People estimate that the local economy lost almost 3 billion dollars. Many families lost their livelihoods.

Oil Spills

1. **Fill in each blank with the correct term from the list below.**

feathers	gills	surface	Exxon Valdez
phytoplankton	oil tankers	jobs	bald eagles

a) When [＿＿＿＿＿＿＿＿] have an accident at sea, a lot of oil can spill out.

b) An oil slick travels on the [＿＿＿＿＿＿＿＿] of the ocean.

c) When oil sticks to birds' [＿＿＿＿＿＿＿＿], the birds cannot fly.

d) Fish cannot breathe when oil sticks to their [＿＿＿＿＿＿＿＿].

e) [＿＿＿＿＿＿＿＿] provide energy for all the animals in the ocean ecosystem.

f) The tanker [＿＿＿＿＿＿＿＿] spilled millions of gallons of oil on the Alaskan coast in 1989.

g) The Exxon Valdez oil spill caused many fishermen to lose their [＿＿＿＿＿＿＿＿].

h) The shore where the Exxon Valdez oil spill reached was home to birds such as [＿＿＿＿＿＿＿＿].

2. **On the lines below, list _five_ animals that were harmed by the Exxon Valdez oil spill.**

_____

_____

_____

_____

_____

 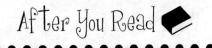

Oil Spills

3. Explain why an oil spill is so harmful to animals. Give examples to support your reasoning.

_____

_____

_____

4. Explain how people can be harmed by oil spills.

_____

_____

_____

Extension & Application

5. Learn more about the lessons people learned from the Exxon Valdez oil spill. Choose **one** of the topics below, or write your own topic. If you write your own topic, show it to your teacher before you start your research. Possible topics:

- How have laws that govern oil shipping changed since the Exxon Valdez spill?
- What did people learn about how to care for birds during an oil spill?
- What did people learn about how to care for ocean mammals during an oil spill?
- What new technologies did people develop to stop oil spills from spreading?
- What new technologies did people develop to make oil tankers safer?
- What did people learn about how to help habitats recover from an oil spill?

Use the Internet or library resources to find the answers to your questions. CREATE A POSTER to share the information you learned. Your poster should contain:

- A brief title that explains your topic
- Pictures or diagrams that explain your topic
- A short written answer to your topic question

Present your poster to the class, and explain what you learned during your research. Display the posters around your school.

NAME: _____

Radioactive Waste

1. Have you ever heard the word **radioactive**? What do you think the meaning of this word might be?

_____

_____

_____

2. Use a dictionary to look up the word NUCLEAR. Write the definition on the lines below. The definition of **nuclear** is:

_____

_____

_____

3. Fill in each blank with the correct term from the list below. You may use a dictionary to help you.

X-rays	CAT-scan	syringe	fuel rod
landfill	barrier	uranium	

a) A [_____] is a place where waste is buried.

b) [_____] are used to see if you have a broken bone.

c) A [_____] places medicine into the body.

d) Radioactive material used in a nuclear power plant is contained in a [_____].

e) A [_____] can make a picture of organs and tissues inside the body.

f) [_____] ore is used as a source of radioactive materials.

g) A [_____] stops things from going in or out.

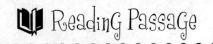
Radioactive Waste

What are radioactive materials?

You may have learned that all matter is made from tiny particles called **atoms**. The center of an atom is called a **nucleus** (plural *nuclei*). The nucleus contains even tinier particles. In some **radioactive** substances, the nuclei break down and release particles. The particles contain large amounts of energy, and can harm the tissues of living things.

People use radioactive materials for many different purposes. In medicine, radioactive materials are used in equipment for seeing inside the body, such as X-rays and CAT-scans. Radioactive substances are also used to treat cancers. In nuclear power plants, radioactive substances are used to produce large amounts of energy. This energy is used to make electricity to power cities and towns.

Describe the meaning of the term *radioactive*.

_____

_____

What is radioactive waste?

Radioactive waste comes from three main sources. First, radioactive minerals must be mined from the earth. These materials include ores such as **uranium**. Some of the leftover materials from the mining can be radioactive. Second, waste is made when radioactive substances are used in medicine and industry. The substances themselves can become waste after they are used. Materials that come into contact with radioactivity can also become radioactive. These materials are called *low-level* radioactive waste, and include things like hospital sheets, gloves, and syringes. The third source of radioactive waste is the radioactive **fuel rods** used in nuclear power plants. After a fuel rod is used for a period of time, it does not produce enough energy to make it useful for making electricity. However, the fuel rod is still very radioactive. Waste fuel rods are called *high-level* radioactive waste.

Radioactive Waste

What happens to radioactive waste?

By their nature, radioactive substances break down. Some radioactive substances break down quickly; others can take millions of years. Radioactive waste must be kept away from people and wildlife during the time when it is still breaking down and releasing harmful radioactive energy.

Waste materials from uranium mines are usually left at the site of the mine. The mine operators contain the waste in barriers that keep the waste away from groundwater. The mine operators must test the air, soil, and water around the mine for many years to be sure that no radioactive wastes are seeping out.

Low-level radioactive wastes are either stored at the place where they were used, or they are brought to special radioactive waste facilities. Most low-level radioactive waste breaks down quickly. It is stored in special containers that do not allow radioactive energy to get out. After a few years, most of the radioactive energy has been released, and the waste material can be safely buried in a landfill.

STOP

Describe how low-level radioactive waste is handled.

_____

_____

High-level radioactive waste creates big problems. Waste fuel rods can release large amounts of harmful radiation for thousands of years. Finding safe places away from people to place these rods is extremely difficult. The places must not experience earthquakes, which can crack containers. They must not be near sources of drinking water. People do not want high level radioactive waste buried near their homes. There is always a risk that containers will leak over thousands of years.

High-level radioactive waste can contaminate huge areas in a nuclear accident or explosion. In 1986, the world's worst nuclear accident happened in a power plant in **Chernobyl**, in the former Soviet Union. An explosion sent high level radioactive materials twenty miles in each direction. Over 300,000 people had to move away from the area. High levels of certain cancers have been found in the area.

Radioactive Waste

1. Circle the word **TRUE** if the statement is TRUE or Circle the word **FALSE** if it is FALSE.

   A) Radioactive substances are used in hospitals.
   >   **TRUE**   **FALSE**

   B) Hospital gloves that have touched radioactive substances must be handled as radioactive waste.
   >   **TRUE**   **FALSE**

   C) Uranium ore is high-level radioactive waste.
   >   **TRUE**   **FALSE**

   D) Radioactive substances can be used in power plants to make electricity.
   >   **TRUE**   **FALSE**

   E) High-level radioactive waste must be disposed of in a landfill.
   >   **TRUE**   **FALSE**

   F) Over 300,000 people had to be moved after the Chernobyl nuclear power plant exploded.
   >   **TRUE**   **FALSE**

   G) Radioactive substances can cause cancer.
   >   **TRUE**   **FALSE**

2. On the lines below, describe **four** ways that people use radioactive substances.

   _____

   _____

   _____

   _____

3. **Circle** the examples of high-level radioactive waste.

   used fuel rods   old X-ray machines   syringes used for cancer treatment

   fallout from a nuclear explosion   wastewater from a uranium mine

   uranium ore   hospital gowns used for CAT-scan patients

Radioactive Waste

4. Explain the difference between **low-level** radioactive waste and **high-level** radioactive waste.

_____

_____

_____

5. Explain why **disposing** of high-level radioactive waste causes so many problems.

_____

_____

_____

Extension & Application

6. Nuclear power plants were once thought to be a good source of electricity, because they do not create any air pollution. However, disposing of fuel rods has become such a big problem, that many people think nuclear power plants are no longer a good solution.

Learn more about the problems of disposing of fuel rods in your country. Use the Internet and library resources to find answers to the following questions.

- Are there nuclear power plants in your country?
- How are the used fuel rods disposed of now?
- Does your country have any plans for permanent fuel rod disposal sites?
- What are the problems that your country faces in finding permanent fuel rod disposal sites?
- How do citizens in your country feel about planned fuel rod disposal sites?
- What are the problems in transporting used fuel rods from nuclear power plants to the disposal sites?
- What are the problems with protecting fuel rod disposal sites?

Now, WRITE AN OPINION PAPER about nuclear energy and fuel rod disposal. In an opinion paper, you state your **opinions** and ideas, and support them with **facts**. The introduction of the paper should outline the facts of used fuel rod disposal, the problems your country faces, and any plans your country has to solve these problems. Then, in the body of the paper, state your opinion about the best way your country can dispose of nuclear fuel rods. Support your opinions with evidence from your research. Finally, give a short summary of the issues, and of your opinion about whether nuclear energy is a good solution for providing electricity to growing societies.

NAME: _____

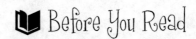

Waste from Natural Disasters

1. In the web below, list **four** examples of natural disasters.

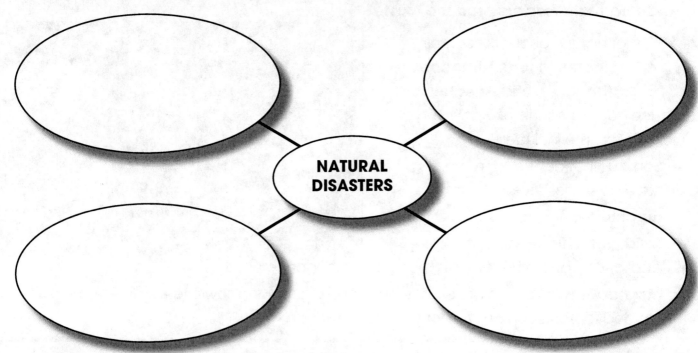

NATURAL DISASTERS

2. Use the words in the list to answer the questions. You may use a dictionary to help you.

tsunami	hurricane	earthquake	debris
sewage	factories	contaminate	disaster

_____ **a)** What type of storm causes very high winds, a lot of rain, and flooding over large areas?

_____ **b)** What is a word for piles of broken parts of buildings, automobiles, and other solid objects?

_____ **c)** What is another word for waste getting into a natural area?

_____ **d)** What event causes the land to shake very hard, and can make buildings fall down?

_____ **e)** What word describes an awful event?

_____ **f)** Which word describes used water from homes and buildings that contains human waste?

_____ **g)** What is a large tidal wave that can be caused by an earthquake?

_____ **h)** What are large buildings where products are made from raw materials?

NAME: _____

Waste from Natural Disasters

How do natural disasters produce waste?

Major natural disasters, such as **hurricanes**, **floods**, **tornadoes**, **earthquakes**, and **tsunamis**, can produce huge amounts of waste very quickly. This waste includes:

- construction **debris**, from buildings that have been destroyed;
- **organic matter**, from downed trees;
- **solid waste**, from cars, furniture, appliances, and other objects that can no longer be used;
- **hazardous waste**, from broken sewage lines, overflowing sewage treatment plants, flooded factories, and hazardous waste dumps.

STOP

Describe the types of waste natural disasters can produce.

_____

_____

How does waste from natural disasters cause harm?

Waste from natural disasters can cause many problems. The first thing to do after a natural disaster is to rescue people. Large piles of debris can make people difficult to find. Debris can bury people and cause dangerous conditions for rescue workers.

Hazardous waste can make people sick. When a large area is flooded, such as after a large hurricane or tsunami, the flood waters can contain hazardous waste. Rescue workers and people who were hurt in or stranded by the disaster can be in contact with flood waters for many days. People in contact with flood waters can get sick from bacterial diseases. They may also take in harmful chemicals that can cause problems years later.

After people are rescued from the disaster area, the solid waste problems can take years to clean up. Large piles of debris are still left in New Orleans from Hurricane Katrina in 2005 and in areas of Asia hit by the tsunami in 2004. Toxic waste and oil spills can harm habitats all around a natural disaster, killing wildlife and **contaminating** drinking water.

NAME: _____

Waste from Natural Disasters

1. Circle the word **TRUE** if the statement is TRUE **or** Circle the word **FALSE** if it is FALSE.

   A) Debris left after a natural disaster can be dangerous for rescue workers.

   TRUE   **FALSE**

   B) Downed trees are an example of hazardous waste left after a natural disaster.

   TRUE   **FALSE**

   C) Flood waters can contain harmful bacteria from sewage.

   TRUE   **FALSE**

   D) All of the debris from Hurricane Katrina in 2005 has been disposed of in landfills.

   TRUE   **FALSE**

   E) Large piles of debris are still left from the 2004 Asian tsunami.

   TRUE   **FALSE**

2. **Use the graphic organizer to list four examples of each kind of waste from natural disasters.**

Examples of construction debris:

1. _____
2. _____
3. _____
4. _____

Examples of organic waste that might be left after a hurricane:

1. _____
2. _____
3. _____
4. _____

Waste from Natural Disasters

Examples of hazardous waste:

1. _____
2. _____
3. _____
4. _____

Examples of solid waste that might be left after flood waters dry up:

1. _____
2. _____
3. _____
4. _____

After You Read 📖

Waste from Natural Disasters

3. What do you think are the **most dangerous** types of waste after a natural disaster? Include facts to support your answer.

_____

_____

_____

4. Why do you think it takes so many years to clean up all of the waste from a large natural disaster, like *Hurricane Katrina* or the *Asian Tsunami*?

_____

_____

_____

Extension & Application

5. Learn more about efforts to **clean up** after major natural disasters. Choose one large natural disaster, such as:

- **The 2005 Hurricane Katrina**
- **The 2004 Asian Tsunami**
- **The 2005 Pakistani Earthquake**

You may choose one of your own, but check with your teacher before beginning your research.

Using the Internet or library resources, find out how communities have been dealing with the waste problems left by the natural disaster that affected them. Make a chart like the one below, listing the main problems, what has been done to address the problems, and what still needs to be done.

Name of natural disaster: _____ **Date it occurred:** _____

Waste Problem Caused by the Disaster	What has been done to fix the problem so far?	What still needs to be done to fix the problem?

NAME: _____

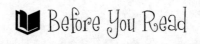

Space Junk

1. What types of <u>objects</u> have humans launched into space?

_____

_____

_____

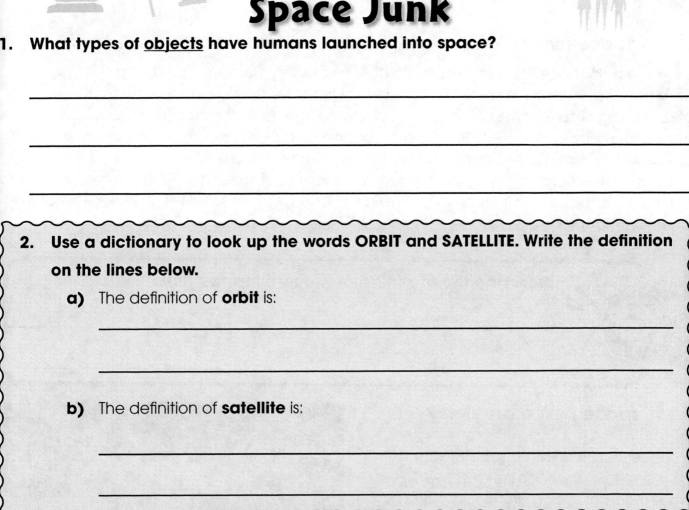

2. Use a dictionary to look up the words ORBIT and SATELLITE. Write the definition on the lines below.

   a) The definition of **orbit** is:

   _____

   _____

   b) The definition of **satellite** is:

   _____

   _____

3. Match word to its meaning. You may use a dictionary to help you.

1 weather	costs a lot of money	**A**
2 passenger	the movement of air and water in Earth's atmosphere	**B**
3 expensive	people talking or sending messages to each other	**C**
4 telescope	a tool used to see objects that are very far away	**D**
5 communications	a person who travels in a vehicle	**E**

Space Junk

What is space junk?

Objects in space that orbit Earth are called **satellites**. Humans have been sending satellites into space since 1957. Since that time, the space around Earth has been getting filled with human-made waste, sometimes called **space junk.** Space junk comes from many sources. Satellites travel to space on rockets. Usually, more than one rocket is used for each satellite. As each rocket is used up, it simply drops off the satellite. If the satellite is high enough above Earth, the rocket stays in orbit instead of falling to the ground. Other types of space junk include old, unused spy and weather satellites; and small pieces of spacecraft that break off in space.

Describe the meaning of the term *space junk.*

_____

_____

Why is space junk a problem?

If a space craft is hit by a piece of space junk, the space craft can be destroyed. Even a small piece of space junk could punch a hole in the wall of a **shuttle** or **space station**, putting the lives of human **passengers** at risk. Space junk could destroy expensive **robotic missions** to other planets, space **telescopes**, and important communications and weather satellites in orbit around Earth.

It is the job of the U.S. Space Surveillance network to keep track of the location of all known space junk. Right now, they are tracking 13,000 pieces of space junk larger than four inches (ten centimeters)! The model at the right shows the area where these

objects are located. Many space scientists think that we need to start sending up space clean-up missions to remove larger pieces of space junk.

Space Junk

1. Fill in each blank with the correct term from the list below.

satellites	space junk	rockets	orbit
missions	planets	wall	spacecraft

a) Some space junk is caused by small pieces of [_____] that break off in space.

b) When [_____] finish firing, they fall off.

c) Space junk includes old, unused spy [_____].

d) Small pieces of space junk can put a hole in the [_____] of a space shuttle.

e) Space junk can damage robotic missions to other [_____].

f) Many space scientists think that we need to send clean-up

[_____] to take down large pieces of space junk.

g) All of the unused waste objects orbiting Earth are [_____].

h) Space junk is in [_____] around Earth.

2. On the lines below, list _five_ examples of space junk.

1. _____

2. _____

3. _____

4. _____

3. _____

Space Junk

3. **Explain why space junk can be dangerous. Give examples to support your reasoning.**

_____

_____

_____

_____

4. **Write your ideas about how people can solve the problem of space junk.**

_____

_____

_____

_____

Extension & Application

5. **Make a model of space junk!**

Materials you can use for this project include:

- clay
- paper
- toothpicks
- wire
- aluminum foil

Scientists are tracking more than 13,000 pieces of space junk in orbit around Earth! This space junk includes everything from large, unused satellites to small pieces of insulation.

Research additional examples of space junk. Find photographs of satellites and rocket boosters, so that you have some idea of what space junk might look like. Then, **create a three-dimensional model of Earth with space junk in orbit.** Be creative! Since you will not be able to make 13,000 pieces of space junk, you should include a key that shows how many actual pieces of space junk one of your model pieces represents. For example, if your model includes 130 pieces of space junk, each piece in the model represents 100 actual pieces of space junk.

Display your model in class.

NAME: _____

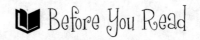

The Cost of Waste

1. Do you think it costs more money to make cans from aluminum that is <u>mined</u> from the earth, or from aluminum that is <u>recycled</u> from cans and other waste objects? Explain your reasoning.

_____

_____

_____

_____

2. Explain the difference between activities that are **SUSTAINABLE** and activities that are **UNSUSTAINABLE**. You may use a dictionary to help you.

_____

_____

_____

_____

3. Match word to its meaning. You may use a dictionary to help you.

1	recycle	groups of people living near each other	A
2	industry	use the material from one object to make another object	B
3	generations	traveling for fun	C
4	communities	businesses related to making and selling goods	D
5	tourism	groups of people who are descended from people living today	E

📖 Reading Passage

The Cost of Waste

What is bio-economics?

Long ago, people often moved into a new territory and quickly used up resources in an **unsustainable** way. They cut trees quickly and used up whole forests. They mined for gold and silver, and left large areas filled with waste. People made money, or **profits**, on the resources, but they did not create industries that would last for many generations. They also did not think about the cost of having to replant and repair habitats, and clean up waste. Now, people are beginning to understand that the money made on natural resources is only part of the picture. The way people take resources from the environment also ends up costing money.

Bio-economics is the study of both the costs and profits of natural resource use. Bio-economics uses both **biology**, the study of living things, and **economics**, the study of money. Bio-economics can help communities plan how to best use their resources. It can help answer questions like, "will we make more money cutting this forest and selling the timber, or using the forest for tourism and sustainable forest products, like nuts and medicines?"

STOP

Describe the meaning of the term _bio-economics_.

_____

_____

What are the bio-economical costs of waste?

Bio-economics has a huge effect on how communities handle their waste. In communities that have few resources, recycling and reusing is a way of life. Very little gets thrown away. But by the middle 1900s, many North American communities became wealthy. Most areas collected only trash, and buried everything in landfills.

Now, people have learned that the bio-economic costs of throwing away useful materials are too high. Activities like mining and cutting trees costs a lot of money in the long run. Recycling materials like plastics, paper, glass, and metals often costs less than getting new materials from nature. Now, many North American communities recycle most of their solid waste.

NAME: _____

The Cost of Waste

1. **Use the words in the list to answer the questions.**

economics	profits	biology	wealthy
landfills	bio-economics	resources	

_____ **a)** What is the study of living things?

_____ **b)** What are things in nature that people use to make products?

_____ **c)** What is the study of money?

_____ **d)** What is the study of both the costs and profits of natural resource use?

_____ **e)** What is the name for money that is made in business?

_____ **f)** What is the name of places where trash is buried?

_____ **g)** What is the term for having a lot of money and resources?

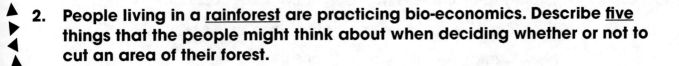

2. **People living in a <u>rainforest</u> are practicing bio-economics. Describe <u>five</u> things that the people might think about when deciding whether or not to cut an area of their forest.**

1) _____

2) _____

3) _____

4) _____

5) _____

The Cost of Waste

3. **Explain why considering the bio-economical cost of an activity is smarter than considering only the profits of that activity.**

_____

_____

_____

_____

4. **Explain why recycling has a lower bio-economical cost than throwing away waste in a landfill.**

_____

_____

_____

_____

Extension & Application

5. **Evaluate** the bio-economical costs of resource use at your home, school, or community. Possible topics include the bio-economical costs of:

- throwing away trash at your home or school

- energy use at your home or school

- land use in your city or town

- industries in your region

Write a topic of your choice and show it to your teacher before going forward.

Research any direct costs and profits associated with the resource use. Then, brainstorm a list of possible additional costs to the environment or human communities that the resource use might have over time. Think of alternative ways to use the resource that might lessen bio-economical costs.

On a large poster board, CREATE A 3-COLUMN CHART to display your bio-economical cost evaluation. The chart headings should be: **Bio-economical costs** (include direct and future costs), **Profits**, and **Lower Cost Alternatives**.

NAME: _____

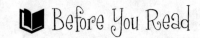

Waste Management Success Stories

1. **Can you think of ways that your school or town could better manage waste? Write your ideas.**

_____

_____

_____

_____

2. **Explain the difference between the act of composting and the material compost. You may use a dictionary to help you.**

_____

_____

_____

_____

3. **Fill in each blank with the correct word from the list below. You may use a dictionary to help you.**

disposable	reduction	compost
biogas	incinerator	natural

a) _____ facilities turn food waste into a source of fuel.

b) If you lessen the amount of waste you throw away, you are practicing waste

_____.

c) Trash is burned in an _____.

d) _____ materials come from plants, animals, or the earth.

e) Worms help turn plant waste into nutrient-rich _____.

f) Products that are used once and then thrown away are _____.

Waste Management Success Stories

People all over the world must learn to manage waste in a way that is sustainable to both the environment and the community. Communities can learn new ways of doing things that keep people and wildlife healthier, and cost less money, too!

How have schools learned to manage waste?

A big source of waste in schools is made during lunch. Lunch waste includes uneaten food, wrappers, and other disposable containers. Many schools have learned ways to lessen lunch waste and save money on garbage collection. One California school even learned how to make money with their lunch waste!

Sixth grade students at Westside Elementary School in Northern California, U.S.A., lead their school's program to reduce lunch waste. They help remind younger students to bring food in reusable containers and to place all recyclable materials in a recycling bin. At lunch, students place all of their food scraps into worm bins. The worms quickly compost students' food waste. Students sell their nutrient-rich compost at a local garden store. Each year, they raise $500 to $1,000 by selling their compost!

Describe two things students can do to lessen the amount of lunch waste.

_____

_____

Schools all over North America are reducing their waste. Students learn to reduce, reuse, recycle, and compost. Canadian schools celebrate Waste Reduction week every year. Schools, along with business and other community groups, are challenged to meet or beat waste reduction goals. Schools across the United States also participate in local and regional waste reduction contests. The practices that students learn during these special events carry over into everyday life. Many students report that their whole family begins to reduce waste at home, too!

Waste Management Success Stories

How can communities reduce waste?

Communities all over the world have waste management problems. As communities grow and make more waste, people often decide to build new waste disposal facilities, such as landfills and incinerators. However, more communities are making the choice to face waste management problems in a new way. Many communities are setting the goal of **zero waste**.

Zero waste is the goal of sending **_nothing at all_** to a landfill or incinerator. Everything used in the community must be reused, recycled, or composted. To do this, communities need to be very creative. One community practicing zero waste is the fishing village of Kovalam, in Kerala, India.

Describe the meaning of the term <u>zero waste</u>.

_____

_____

How does Kovalam practice zero waste?

Many people from all over the world came to visit Kovalam for its beautiful beaches on the shores of the Arabian Sea. However, when people visited, they brought a lot of waste. Over many years, the small village became overrun with waste. Waste piled up on beaches and along side roads. Some people suggested building an incinerator to burn the waste. But other people did not want the air pollution that comes from burning waste.

Instead, the people of Kovalam made the choice to practice zero waste. The people make and sell reusable containers for water and food out of natural materials such as coconut shells. They built a biogas plant that uses food waste to make fuel. They collect and recycle glass, metal, and plastic. Many farmers in the area have made the choice to stop using harmful pesticides and fertilizers. Now, Kovalam is a model for communities around the world that want to get rid of waste without harming people, wildlife, or beautiful natural places.

After You Read

Waste Management Success Stories

1. Write one of the place names below on each of the lines to tell <u>where</u> the activity took place. You may use each place name more than once.

Kovalam	Westside School, California	Canada

_____ **a)** A biogas facility changes food waste into usable fuel.

_____ **b)** Students sell compost to raise money for their school.

_____ **c)** People make and sell reusable containers out of natural materials.

_____ **d)** Schools participate in Waste Reduction Week.

_____ **e)** Older students help younger students remember to recycle.

_____ **f)** Trash from vacationers built up on the beaches.

2. Fill in each blank with the correct word from the list below.

disposable	compost	worms
pesticides	incinerator	zero waste

a) _____ help break down food waste in a compost bin.

b) Lunch waste includes wrappers and other _____ containers.

c) Communities that set the goal of _____ try not to send anything to landfills or incinerators.

d) Students at Westside School _____ uneaten food instead of throwing it in the trash.

e) Burning trash in an _____ can cause a lot of air pollution.

f) Farmers near Kovalam have decided to stop using harmful _____.

Waste Management Success Stories

3. How can you <u>apply</u> the lessons people learned in Kovalam, India, to your own town or local community?

_____

_____

_____

_____

4. Could your school have a program like the one at Westside Elementary? Explain how students at your school could change the way your school manages waste.

_____

_____

_____

_____

Extension & Application

5. Have a <u>zero-waste lunch day</u> at your school! First, make posters that explain the ways to lessen lunch waste, including:

- bringing food to school in reusable containers
- recycling all materials that can be recycled
- packing only the amount of food that you will really eat
- bringing uneaten food home to eat later instead of throwing it away

Then, have classrooms **compete** to have the least waste! Ask your principal or parents' group to donate a prize for the winning class. On the zero-waste day, students from each class should throw away their trash in separate class bins. At the end of lunch, a group of students can look in each bin to judge which class had the least trash.

Biomass Product Fair

In this activity, you and your classmates will learn about the many different products that can be made from unused plant parts on farms, or BIOMASS.

FIRST, use the Internet or library resources to research a list of **10 to 20** different products that can be made from biomass. Include fuels, building materials, gardening supplies, and everyday items.

SECOND, have each student in your class choose a product from the list to learn more about. Students may work alone or in teams.

Once you have chosen your product, **research** answers to the following questions:

- What types of agricultural waste are used to make the product?
- How is the product made?
- Do farmers make money selling their waste to the manufacturers of the product?
- What is the product used for?
- Can the product replace similar products made from nonrenewable resources?

If possible, try to get a sample of your product. If that is not possible, get photographs or advertisements.

Make a **poster presentation** that answers all of the questions above and contains photographs of the product and the waste materials used to make it.

THIRD, set up a **Biomass Product Fair** in your classroom or common school area, such as the auditorium. Display the posters and products on tables, and have students stand near their displays to answer questions. Invite students, teachers, parents, and other members of your school community to walk through the Biomass Product Fair.

Nuclear Fuel Debate

Set up a class debate about the use of nuclear energy to make electricity. Nuclear energy has **ADVANTAGES** and **DISADVANTAGES**. It does not create air pollution like burning fossil fuels. It does not add greenhouse gases to the atmosphere. However, it does have the problem of creating radioactive waste.

BEFORE YOU BEGIN

Have students choose whether they will argue **for** or **against** the use of nuclear energy to make electricity. Or, have students draw straws to be randomly assigned to one group or the other.

DO YOUR RESEARCH

Together as a group, research all of the advantages and disadvantages of nuclear energy. Read what experts have to say on both sides of the issue. Find out how much nuclear energy costs compared to other types of energy. Then, try to analyze the bio-economic costs of nuclear energy compared to other types of energy.

Write a list of **five main points** that your group would like to make in the debate. After you write your list, try to think of what the other group might say in response to your points. Talk about how you will respond to arguments about the points you are making.

Choose one person in your group to make each of the points. If there are more people left in your group, choose one person to respond to each of the other team's points.

CONDUCT THE DEBATE

In the debate, each side will have 2 minutes to make each of their points. Teams will take turns. Team A will make their first point, then Team B will have 2 minutes to make an argument against that point. Finally, Team A has one additional minute to respond to Team B's argument. Then, Team B has 2 minutes to make their first point. Team A will have 2 minutes to make an argument against that point. Then, Team B has one additional minute to respond to Team A's argument. This process continues until all of the points have been made.

Zero Waste School Plan

Write a plan to help your school become a **zero waste** community.

RESEARCH YOUR SCHOOL'S WASTE

TAKE A SURVEY of your school's waste. Walk around the school grounds, and visit each of the buildings. In each area, note the following:

- litter
- the main types of waste in trash bins
- the location of recycling bins, what materials can be collected in the bins, and whether they are being used

WRITE YOUR ZERO WASTE PLAN

SUMMARIZE the main types of waste being thrown away at your school. Note any problems with certain kinds of waste becoming litter. Evaluate how well recycling programs are working.

BRAINSTORM a list of ideas about what students, teachers, and staff can do to help lessen the waste that is thrown away at school. Ask the following questions:

- How can people substitute reusable containers and items for disposable ones?
- What can be done to make sure all recyclable materials are placed in the correct recycling bins instead of in the trash?
- What can be done to lessen food waste?
- How can students reuse materials in the classroom?

Write your ideas as a set of ACTION STEPS. For example, "Assign students to help pick up litter in the cafeteria after lunch."

Present your zero waste school plan to students, teachers, and your principal.

Waste Management Success Story Documentary

In this activity, you will work in a small group to create a documentary about a group of people that has come up with creative ways to solve waste management problems.

First, use the Internet or library resources to research communities that have been successful at greatly reducing the waste that they produce. The community you choose might have the goal of **zero waste.** Once you find a community to report on, ask the following questions:

- What was the waste management problem that the community had to begin with?
- How did people come together to make a plan to address the problem?
- What steps did people take first?
- Did people learn to do different things with their waste?
- Did people build new facilities?

Gather any information about the waste management program that you can find.

Second, watch a few documentaries to become familiar with the style. Think about how they are narrated, and how images are used to help the viewer understand the topic.

Third, write and produce a documentary about your community. Write the narration in a clear, descriptive style, and be sure the narrative covers all of the questions above. Plan how you will use images while the narrator is speaking. If possible, try to contact a representative from the community you researched. Ask the representative if you could tape them talking about their community, or if you could use some written quotes in your documentary.

Fourth, using a video camera, tape your documentary. You may want to start and stop the tape each time you change images. You can even record the narration separately and edit the tape together.

Finally, show your documentary in class!

After You Read

Crossword Puzzle!

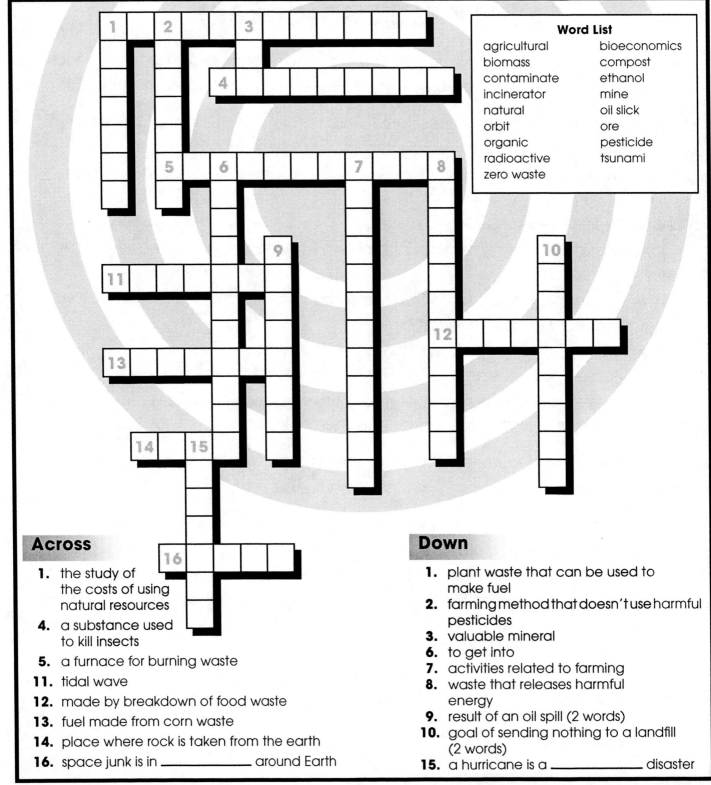

Word List

agricultural	bioeconomics
biomass	compost
contaminate	ethanol
incinerator	mine
natural	oil slick
orbit	ore
organic	pesticide
radioactive	tsunami
zero waste	

Across

1. the study of the costs of using natural resources
4. a substance used to kill insects
5. a furnace for burning waste
11. tidal wave
12. made by breakdown of food waste
13. fuel made from corn waste
14. place where rock is taken from the earth
16. space junk is in _____ around Earth

Down

1. plant waste that can be used to make fuel
2. farming method that doesn't use harmful pesticides
3. valuable mineral
6. to get into
7. activities related to farming
8. waste that releases harmful energy
9. result of an oil spill (2 words)
10. goal of sending nothing to a landfill (2 words)
15. a hurricane is a _____ disaster

Word Search

Find all of the words in the Word Search. Words are written horizontally, vertically, diagonally, and some are even written backwards.

acid	economics	industries	reduce
atom	Exxon Valdez	Kovalam	reuse
biogas	fertilizer	landfill	rock
Chernobyl	fuel rods	mining	space junk
cyanide	fungicide	nuclear	sustainable
debris	habitat	profits	toxic
disposable	hazardous	recycle	uranium

A	D	S	D	F	G	H	J	K	L	R	Z	D	X	C	R	V	R
Z	S	F	E	R	T	I	L	I	Z	E	R	E	G	C	V	O	Q
A	D	U	A	A	Q	S	O	Q	A	D	A	B	Q	A	C	S	W
S	I	N	S	S	W	D	P	W	S	U	S	R	W	K	Q	P	E
D	S	G	S	T	E	F	U	E	D	C	D	I	E	C	W	A	R
F	P	I	D	D	A	G	R	R	R	E	U	S	E	H	E	C	T
G	O	C	F	F	R	I	A	L	F	Z	F	Q	T	E	R	E	Y
H	S	I	G	G	R	H	N	T	A	X	G	W	Y	R	T	J	U
J	A	D	H	P	E	C	I	A	G	N	H	E	U	N	Y	U	I
K	B	E	J	R	C	Y	U	Y	B	C	D	R	I	O	U	N	O
I	L	A	K	O	Y	A	M	U	H	L	J	F	O	B	I	K	P
N	E	S	L	F	C	N	A	N	J	V	E	T	I	Y	O	Q	A
D	H	D	P	I	L	I	S	U	K	B	C	Y	P	L	P	W	S
U	S	A	Q	T	E	D	D	C	L	T	O	M	A	S	L	E	D
S	D	F	B	S	Y	E	F	L	Q	T	N	U	I	D	A	R	F
T	F	G	W	I	U	J	G	E	W	N	O	I	S	N	B	T	G
R	G	H	M	O	T	A	H	A	E	M	M	X	D	F	I	Y	H
I	H	J	E	H	C	A	J	R	R	O	I	O	I	G	O	N	J
E	J	K	R	I	I	K	T	I	T	P	C	P	F	C	G	U	G
S	K	L	D	K	O	V	A	L	A	M	S	Z	G	H	A	I	K
Z	L	H	A	Z	A	R	D	O	U	S	K	X	H	J	S	O	L
X	O	Z	T	J	O	L	X	F	U	E	L	R	O	D	S	P	Z
E	X	X	O	N	V	A	L	D	E	Z	L	C	I	K	S	L	X

Part A

1. Circle the word **TRUE** if the statement is TRUE **or** Circle the word **FALSE** if it is FALSE.   8

A) Corn stalks are an example of agricultural waste
   TRUE   FALSE

B) Hazardous mining waste can contaminate water supplies.
   TRUE   FALSE

C) When oil is spilled from a tanker, it spreads out on the ocean floor.
   TRUE   FALSE

D) High-level radioactive waste can remain harmful for thousands of years.
   TRUE   FALSE

E) Solid waste from Hurricane Katrina is still a problem.
   TRUE   FALSE

F) About 300 pieces of space junk can be found orbiting Earth.
   TRUE   FALSE

G) Bio-economics is the study of how much money it costs to dispose of organic wastes.
   TRUE   FALSE

H) Incinerators can cause air pollution.
   TRUE   FALSE

Part B

Put a check mark (✓) next to the answer that is most correct.   4

1. **Which of these is high-level radioactive waste?**
   - O **A** uranium ore
   - O **B** X-ray machines
   - O **C** cancer medicines
   - O **D** used fuel rods

2. **Which of these substances are found in waste from metal mines?**
   - O **A** acids
   - O **B** oil
   - O **C** sewage
   - O **D** fungicides

3. **Which of these is an example of agricultural waste?**
   - O **A** cyanide
   - O **B** acids
   - O **C** fertilizer
   - O **D** aluminum

4. **Which facility will help a community practice zero waste?**
   - O **A** biogas
   - O **B** incinerator
   - O **C** landfill
   - O **D** nuclear plant

After You Read 📖

Part C # Comprehension Quiz

Answer the questions in complete sentences.

1. Describe **two** ways that farmers can lessen agricultural waste. ②

_____

_____

_____

2. Describe **two** types of mining waste and **compare** the amount of harm each type of waste can cause. ④

_____

_____

_____

3. Explain why an **oil spill** can be so harmful to a shoreline environment. Give examples to support your answer. ③

_____

_____

_____

_____

4. Describe **two** ways that hazardous waste can be released in a natural disaster. ②

_____

_____

_____

5. Compare the **bio-economical cost** of throwing away food waste to composting food waste. ②

_____

_____

_____

SUBTOTAL: /13

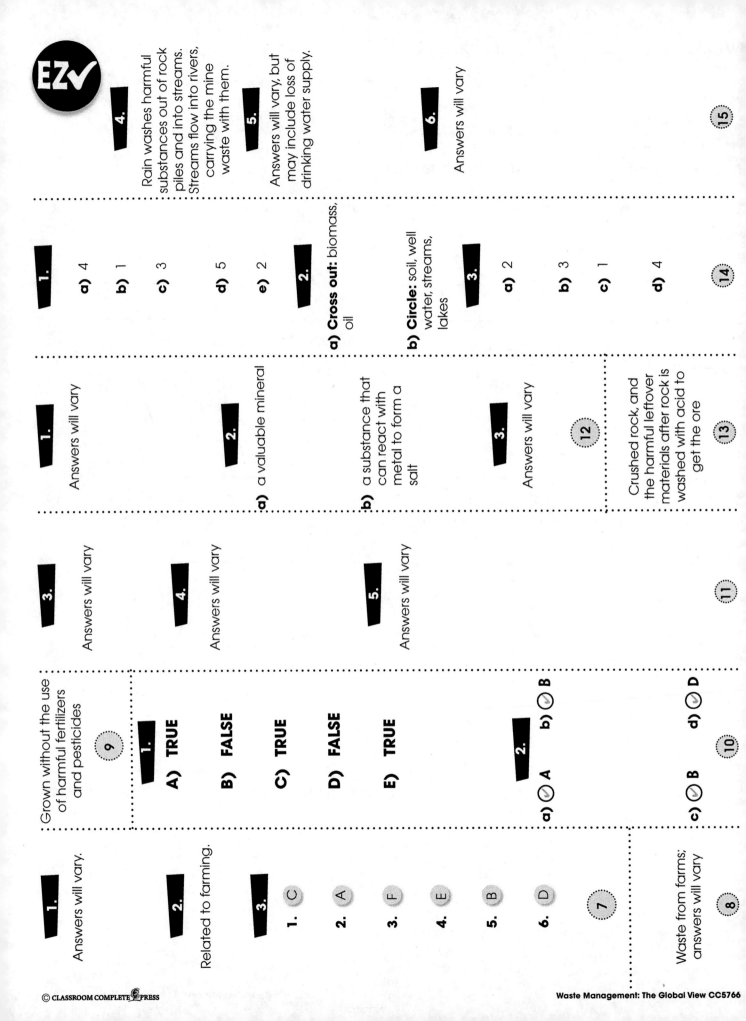

EZ✓

4. Rain washes harmful substances out of rock piles and into streams. Streams flow into rivers, carrying the mine waste with them.

5. Answers will vary, but may include loss of drinking water supply.

6. Answers will vary

1.
a) 4
b) 1
c) 3
d) 5
e) 2

2.
a) **Cross out:** biomass, oil
b) **Circle:** soil, well water, streams, lakes

3.
a) 2
b) 3
c) 1
d) 4

1. Answers will vary

2.
a) a valuable mineral
b) a substance that can react with metal to form a salt

3. Answers will vary

12

13 Crushed rock, and the harmful leftover materials after rock is washed with acid to get the ore

3. Answers will vary

4. Answers will vary

5. Answers will vary

9 Grown without the use of harmful fertilizers and pesticides

1.
A) TRUE
B) FALSE
C) TRUE
D) FALSE
E) TRUE

2.
a) A
b) B
c) B
d) D

10

1. Answers will vary.

2. Related to farming.

3.
1. C
2. A
3. F
4. E
5. B
6. D

7

8 Waste from farms; answers will vary

4. Low-level radioactive waste breaks down faster.

5. High-level radioactive waste takes thousands of years before it will no longer cause harm to people.

6. Answers will vary

24

Placed in special containers that do not allow radioactive energy to escape.

22

1.
A) TRUE
B) TRUE
C) FALSE
D) TRUE
E) FALSE
F) TRUE
G) TRUE

2. Answers will vary

3. Circle: used fuel rods, fallout from a nuclear explosion

23

---

1. Answers will vary

2. Pertaining to processes that happen in the nucleus of an atom.

3.
a) landfill
b) X-rays
c) syringe
d) fuel rod
e) CAT-scan
f) uranium
g) barrier

20

21

Putting out high energy particles from the breakdown of atomic nuclei.

---

3. Answers will vary

4. Answers may include loss of jobs

5. Answers will vary

19

A film of waste oil floating on top of water

17

1.
a) oil tankers
b) surface
c) feathers
d) gills
e) phytoplankton
f) Exxon Valdez
g) jobs
h) bald eagles

2. Answers will vary

18

---

1. The oil floats on the water.

2. Answers will vary

3. A group of living things that interact with each other and the nonliving things around them.

16

1. Answers will vary

2. Activities that are sustainable can continue into the future without using up resources. Activities that are unsustainable cannot continue for long without using up resources.

3.
1. B
2. D
3. E
4. A
5. C

33

3. Answers will vary

4. Answers will vary

5. Answers will vary

32

1.
a) spacecraft
b) rockets
c) satellites
d) wall
e) planets
f) missions
g) space junk
h) orbit

2. Answers will vary

31

1. Answers will vary

2.
a) a circular path
b) an object that orbits a body in space

3.
1. B
2. E
3. A
4. D
5. C

29

Waste objects in orbit around Earth.

30

1.
A) TRUE
B) FALSE
C) TRUE
D) FALSE
E) TRUE

2. Answers will vary

27

3. Answers will vary

4. Answers will vary

5. Answers will vary

28

1. Answers will vary

2.
a) hurricane
b) debris
c) contaminate
d) earthquake
e) disaster
f) sewage
g) tsunami
h) factories

25

Answers will vary

26

Answers will vary
42

Answers will vary
43

Answers will vary
44

Answers will vary
45

3. Answers will vary

4. Answers will vary

5. Answers will vary

41

The goal of sending nothing at all to a landfill or incinerator
39

1.
a) Kovalam
b) Westside School
c) Kovalam
d) Canada
e) Westside School
f) Kovalam

2.
a) worms
b) disposable
c) zero waste
d) compost
e) incinerator
f) pesticides
40

1. Answers will vary

2. Composting is the act of breaking down organic waste. Compost is a nutrient-rich soil that is the product of composting.

3.
a) biogas
b) reduction
c) incinerator
d) natural
e) compost
f) disposable
37

Answers will vary
38

3. Considering profits only looks at the short-term. In the long-term an activity can have a lot more costs.

4. When waste is thrown away, new materials must be mined or cut to make new products. Making new products from old materials by recycling has a much lower cost to the environment.

5. Answers will vary

36

The study of both the costs and profits of natural resource use
34

1.
a) biology
b) resources
c) economics
d) bio-economics
e) profits
f) landfills
g) wealthy

2. Answers will vary

35

Part C

1. Answers will vary, but may include using waste plant parts to make fuel, and choosing organic farming methods.

2. Broken-up rock, which is not harmful; the material left after acid has been used to separate metal from the rest of the rock, which is very harmful.

3. The oil spreads over a great distances and covers animals. Examples will vary.

4. Answers will vary.

5. Answers will vary.

49

Part A

A) TRUE

B) TRUE

C) FALSE

D) TRUE

E) TRUE

F) FALSE

G) FALSE

H) TRUE

Part B

1) D   2) A

3) C   4) A

48

Word Search Answers

47

Across

1. bioeconomics

4. pesticide

5. incinerator

11. tsunami

12. compost

13. ethanol

14. mine

16. orbit

Down

1. biomass

2. organic

3. ore

6. contaminate

7. agricultural

8. radioactive

9. oil slick

10. zero waste

15. natural

46

Agricultural Waste
(Farmer Spraying Pesticide on Rice Field)

Agricultural Waste

(Farmer Spraying Pesticide on Rice Field)

Mining Waste

(Polluted River Downstream from Operating Mine)

• • • • • • • • • • • • • • • • • • • • • • • • • • • •

Nuclear Power Plant

Nuclear Power Plant

Ethanol Plant
(Converting Corn into Fuel)